My Kind of Music

BOOK 2

Elementary to Late Elementary

Kevin Olson

Note from the Composer

Isn't it great when you find a piece of music that perfectly captures who you are, what you like, and how you think? Maybe you really like the title, or the melody stays in your head all day, or maybe it's just simply a blast to play! When you feel that special connection with a musical work, you want to play it and hear it over and over again. I created these compositions with you in mind, hoping that some of them would connect with you in that exciting way. Best wishes in your discovery of pieces about which you could exclaim, "Hey! That's my kind of music!"

Kevin Olson

Contents

Somethin' Spicy

The "spiciness" of this piece comes from the short staccatos and accents!
Also, when you see the time signature changes in measure 17 and beyond, make sure to keep the quarter note beat steady.

Kevin Olson

Fast and peppery! (♩ = 208 or faster)

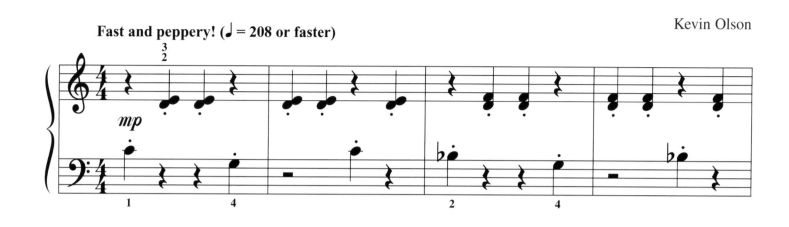

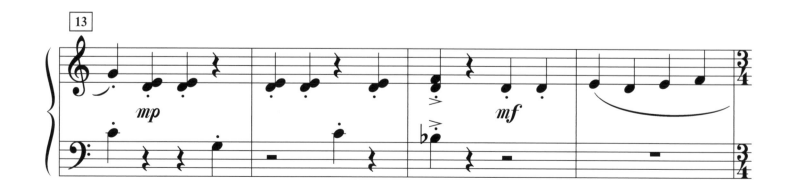

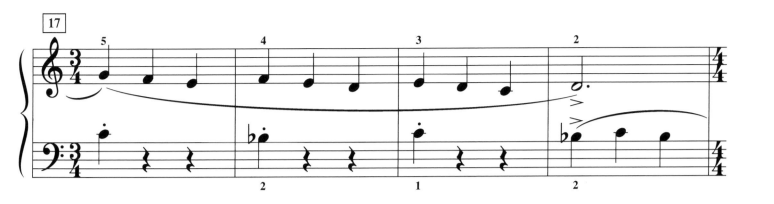

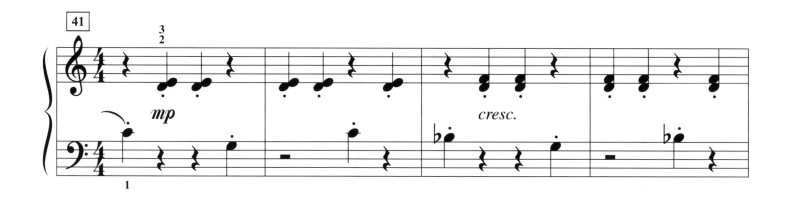

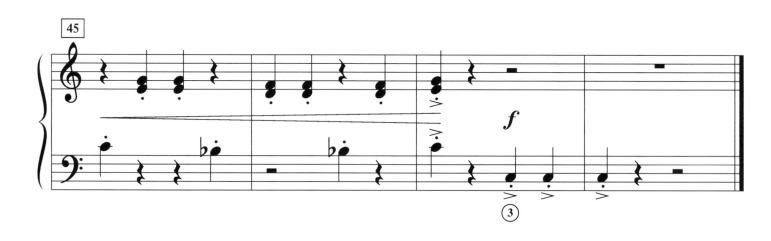

Too Cool

This bluesy piece should sound lazy and relaxed. Don't lose the "coolness" by going too fast!

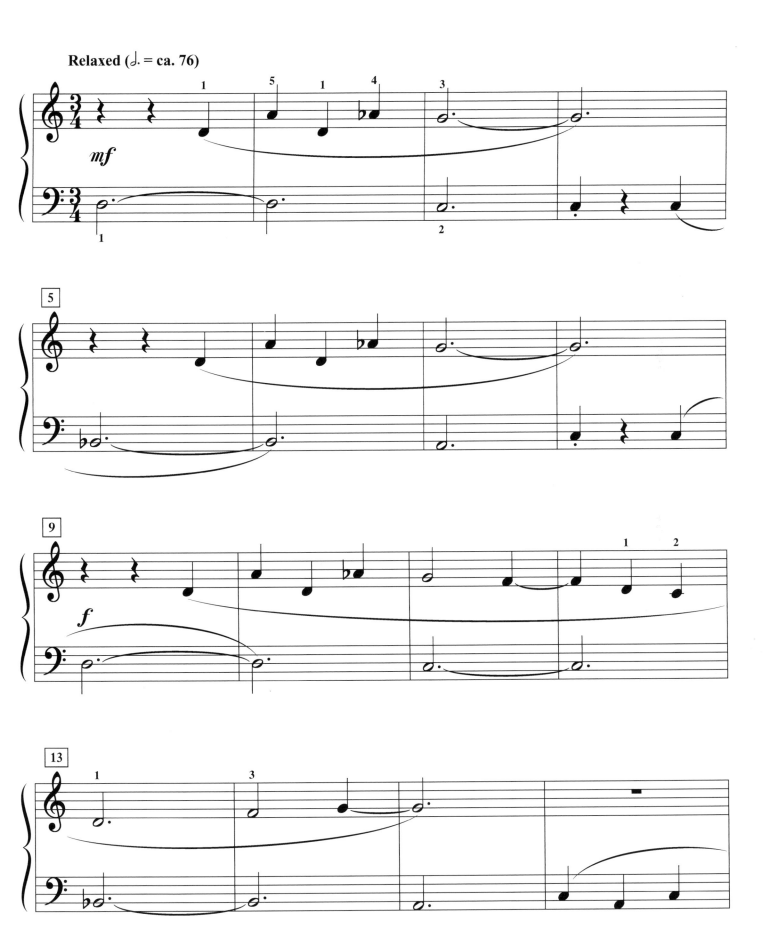

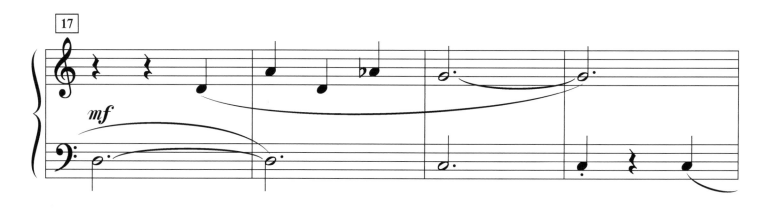

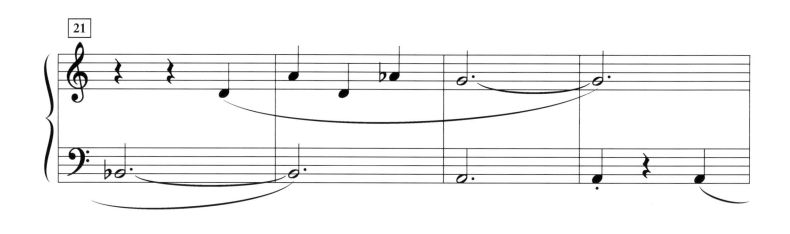

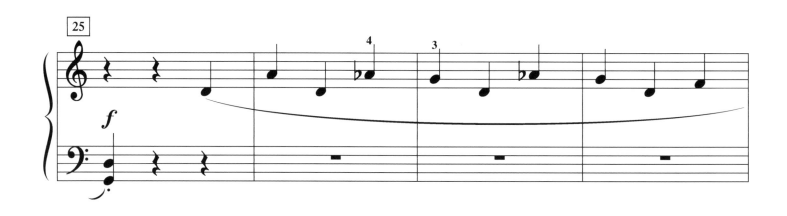

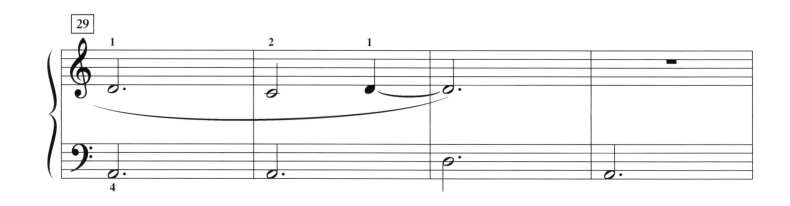

9

FJH1704

Saturday Surfers

*This surfer song begins with two ideas: long half-note power chords in the right hand
and short quarter-note lines in the left hand. Where do the hands switch these ideas?*

A Sudden Storm

In the Midwest, where I live, storms can literally come out of nowhere.
Capture the scene of dark skies and swirling winds by keeping a steady, energetic beat.
What images come to mind when you play the staccatos in measures 17-28?

Driving (♩. = **92 or faster**)

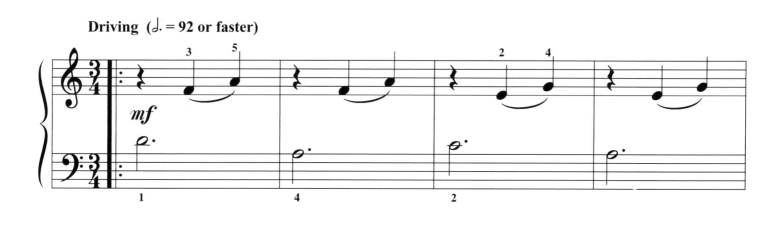

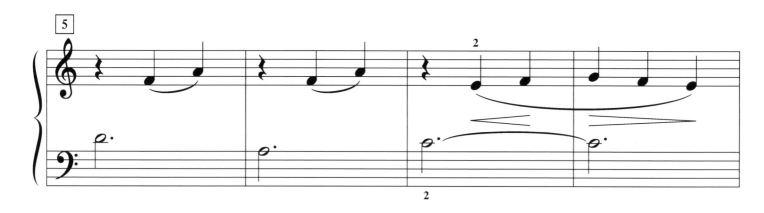

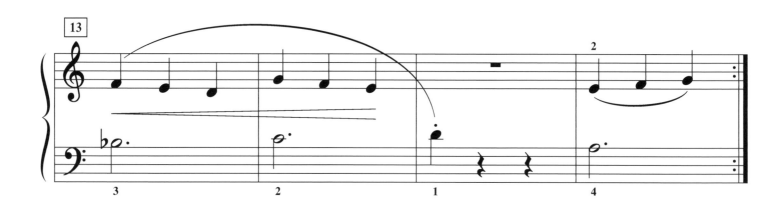

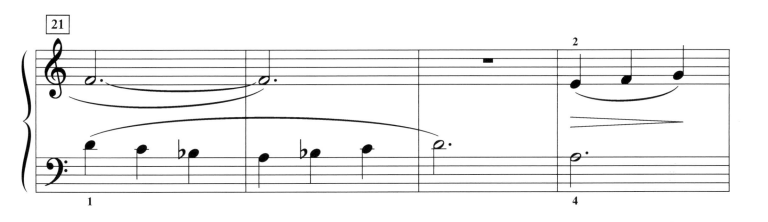

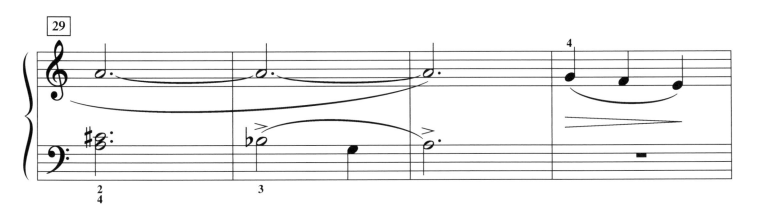

Midnight Mist

You can portray the eeriness of mist in the darkness by playing a clean, careful pedal and following the dynamics exactly.
What measures are the loudest in this piece?

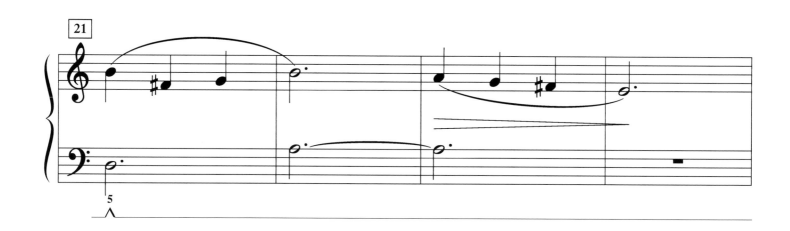

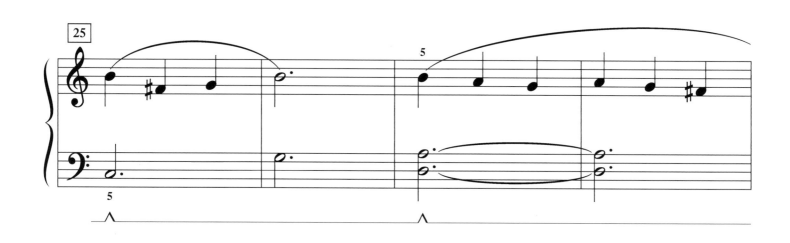

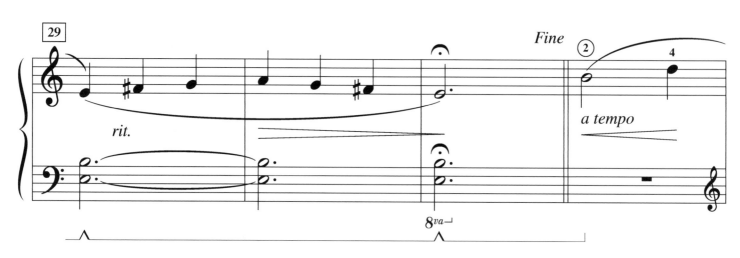

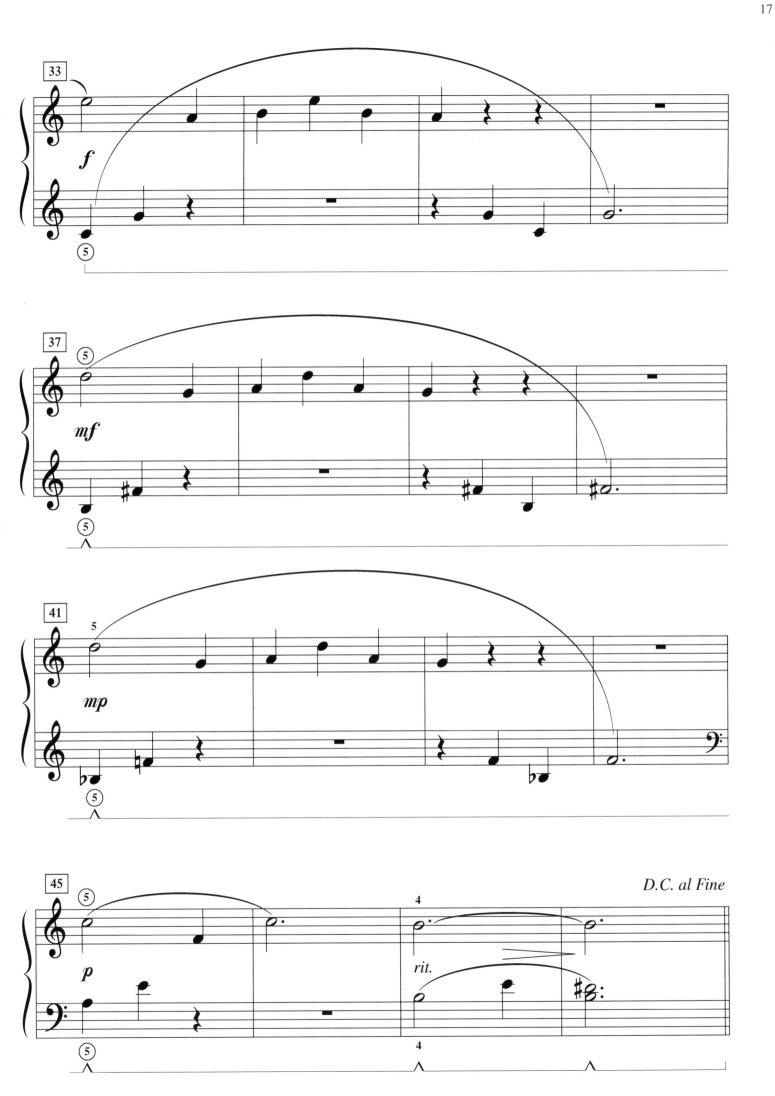

The Old Carousel

To me, nothing says summer like county fairs and old carousels.
Work to create a continuous, legato melody, even when it switches from the left hand to the right.
Don't forget to slow down at the end, as the carousel comes to a halt.

Island Song

If you have a digital piano, try playing this on a "steel drum" or "xylophone" setting
to capture the feel of the Caribbean. The syncopated rhythms in measures 1-2 are tricky,
but once you learn them, they come back again and again.

With a tropical punch! ($\quad$ = 208 or faster)

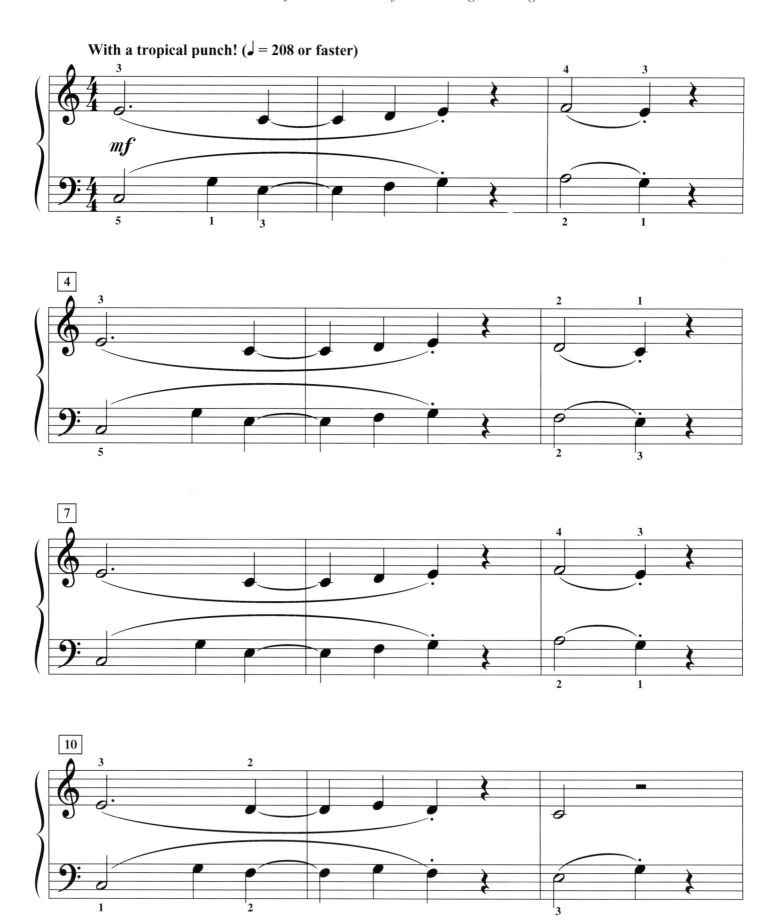

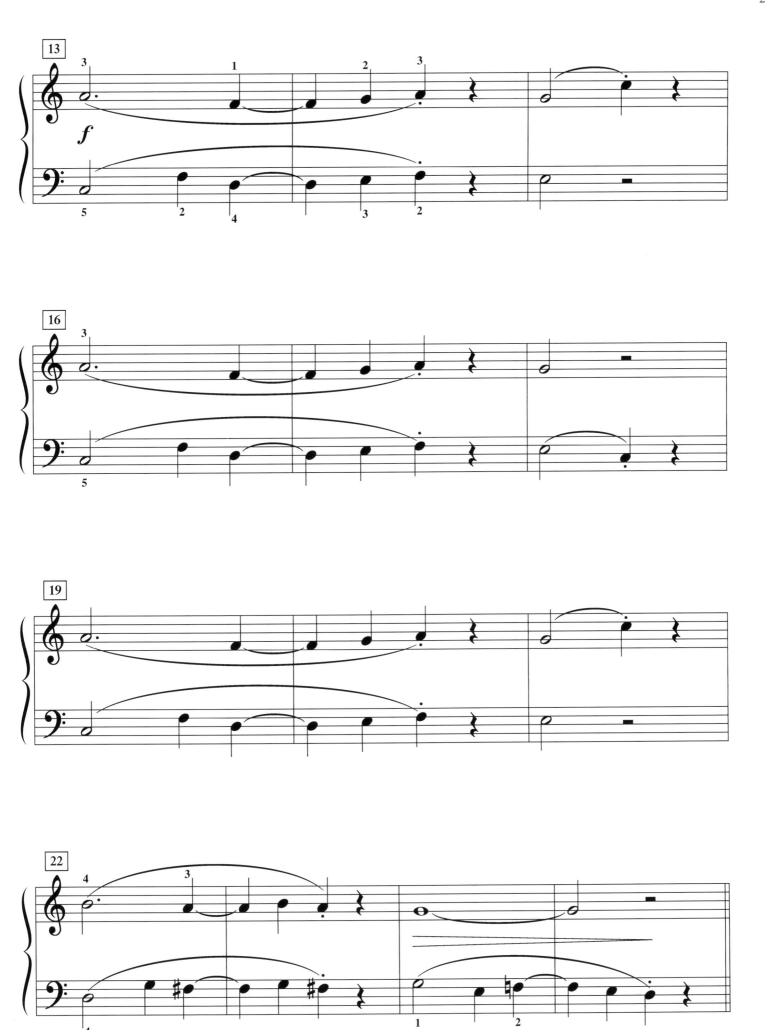

Under Starry Skies

This piece conjures up the tranquility of laying underneath a sky full of stars on a dark summer night.
Notice that the pedal changes each time the left hand moves.
Work to lift and depress the pedal after you play each chord, so it sounds smooth and clear.

Peacefully, not too slowly ($\downarrow$ = ca. 144)

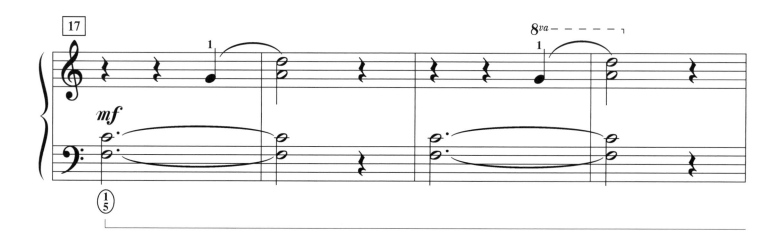

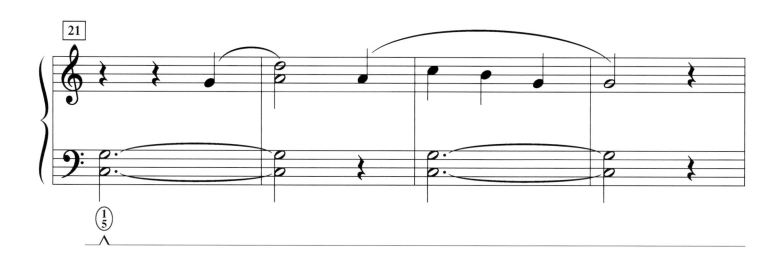

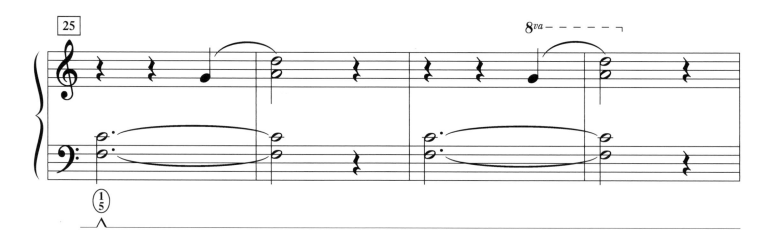

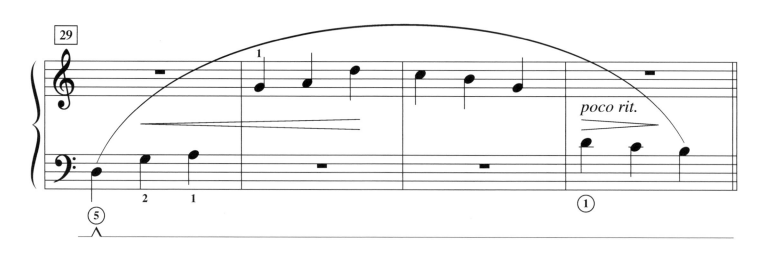

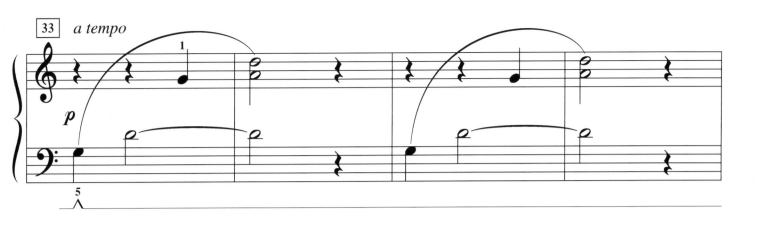

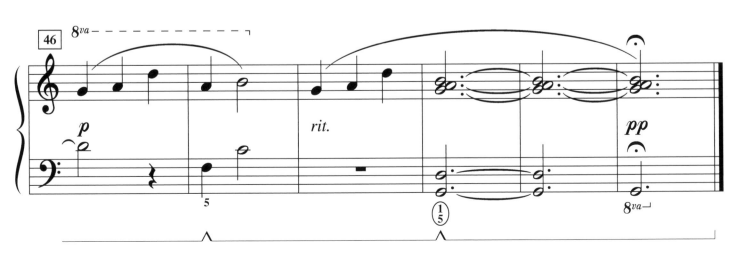

Forest Trails

One of my favorite parts of hiking is discovering new trails that lead to unknown destinations.
This piece captures both the excitement and mystery of uncharted forest trails.
Which hand plays the melody more — the right or the left? Make sure and bring it out, and give it an interesting shape.

Mysteriously (♩ = 200 or faster)

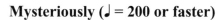

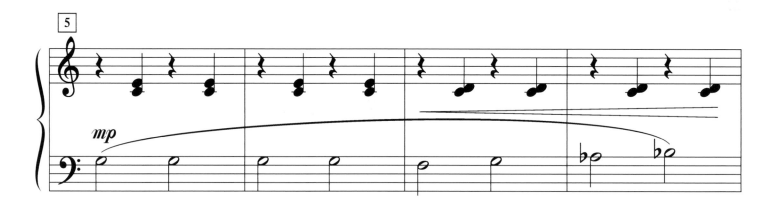

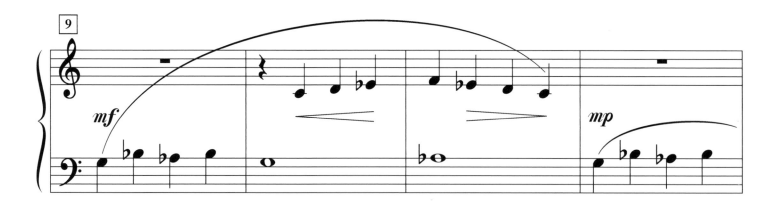

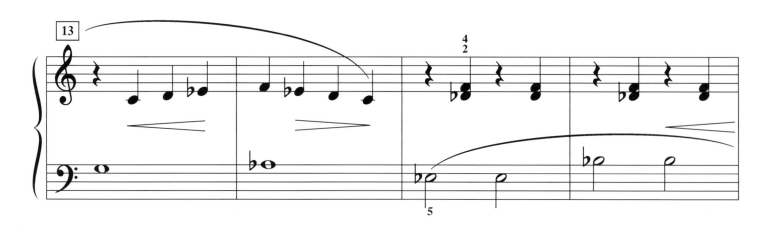

FJH1704

28

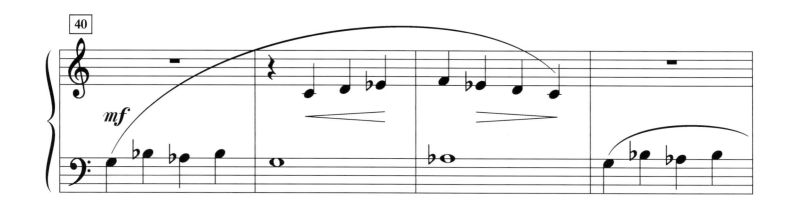

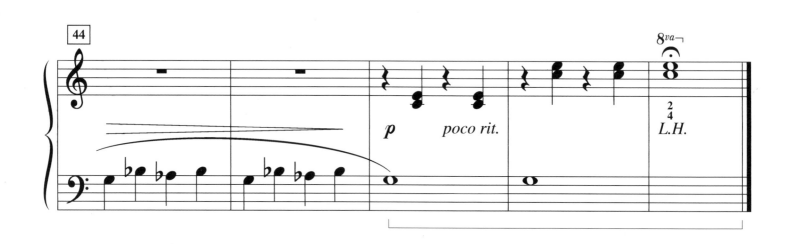

FJH1704